CONTENTS

KV-106-258

Sections marked with this symbol have free audio clips available at www.franklinwatts.co.uk/downloads

Ryan

MEET RYAN, OUR YOUNG REPORTER IN FRANCE

Meet Ryan. He is in France on a special mission. He is going to find out what it is like to go to school in France. He has lots of questions.

What do children wear to school?

What is **la rentrée?**

Do they have school teams or clubs?

Which days do children go to school?

What happens if children don't behave?

Do French children have the same lessons as me?

Read on and find out
the answers to these questions…
and lots more!

BIENVENUE EN FRANCE!

CREST

The little town of Crest is in south-east France. Meet some children who live there.

Léo is 9.

He lives with his mum and dad and his big brother.

He likes sport, music and riding his bike.

He speaks two languages: French and English.

Léo

Francky

Francky is 13.

He lives with his mum and dad.

He hasn't got any brothers and sisters.

He loves playing the drums and reading.

Did you know?

There are three million children between the ages of 8 and 12 in France.

Marie-Lou is 10.

She lives with her mother and her little sister.

Her favourite things are dogs, judo and watching TV.

She is learning English at school.

Marie-Lou

You can practise your French and learn some new words as you find out what these children have to say.

LA RENTRÉE

Today our young reporter is interviewing Marie-Lou. She is busy getting ready to go back to school after the long summer holidays.

Young reporter: **Salut, Marie-Lou! Qu'est-ce que tu fais?**

Marie-Lou: **C'est la rentrée! Je prépare mon cartable.**

Mon école s'appelle l'École primaire Charles Royannez. La maîtresse s'appelle Madame Mercier.

La rentrée is an important day in France. It's the day in early September when children go back to school after the summer holidays. It is the same day for all the schools in the country.

To keep their brains working over the summer, children have summer-holiday activity books (**les cahiers de vacances**).

USEFUL PHRASES

Qu'est-ce que tu fais? What are you doing?   **c'est…** it's…
Je prépare mon cartable. I'm getting my school bag ready.
mon école s'appelle… my school is called…   **la maîtresse** the teacher (in primary school)

In July and August, French school children have a two-month summer break with no school (called **les grandes vacances** or **les vacances d'été**). Marie-Lou loves the summer, but she is looking forward to going back to school too! She'll see all her friends again and she'll be in a new class with a new class teacher.

Marie-Lou walks to school with her friends.

At the end of last term, her teacher gave her a list of all the school equipment she'll need this year – it's three pages long! – and it's important she gets everything exactly right. The school only provides her textbooks (**les manuels**). I noticed that the pages of French exercise books (**les cahiers**) have squares instead of lines. Marie-Lou says this helps to keep her handwriting neat.

LES ANIMAUX EN DANGER

Marie-Lou's **cahier**

Another thing Marie-Lou has to think about is what to wear on her first day back. There is no school uniform in France! Everyone can wear what they like.

What's in Marie-Lou's bag?

a diary (**un agenda**)   an exercise book (**un cahier**)   a folder (**un classeur**)
pencils (**des crayons**)   a pencil case (**une trousse**)   felt-tip pens (**des feutres**)
a rubber (**une gomme**)   a pencil-sharpener (**un taille-crayons**)   a calculator
(**une calculatrice**)   a ruler (**une règle**)   sports gear (**des affaires de sport**)

YOUR TURN

Et toi? Complète.

- *Je m'appelle…*
- *Mon école s'appelle…*
- *La maîtresse (or Le maître*) s'appelle…*

* le maître for a male teacher

Did you spot that there are two different French words for 'a'?

un is for masculine words, **une** is for feminine words. Even objects like a table are either masculine or feminine in French.

GOING TO SCHOOL IN FRANCE

In France, all children between 6 and 16 must go to school.

Most French children go to state schools which are free and open to everyone. The type of school you go to and the class you are in depend mainly on your age. Sometimes, if a pupil hasn't made good progress, he or she has to repeat a year.

Your age		Type of school
2-6	→	**école maternelle** (nursery school)
6-11	→	**école primaire** (primary school)
11-15	→	**collège** (secondary school)
15-18	→	**lycée** (sixth-form college)

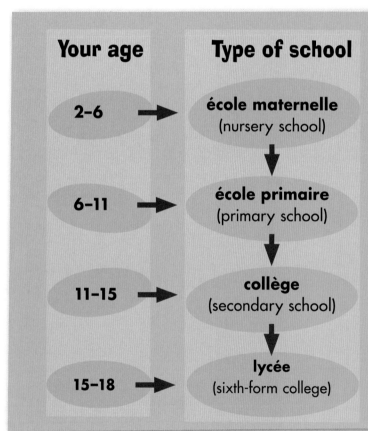

Did you know?

There are some good French films where the action takes place in a school for example **Être et avoir** (*To Be and To Have*), **Les Choristes** (*The Chorus*) and **Entre les Murs** (*The Class*).

Which class?

SCHOOL	CLASS	ABBREVIATION	AGES
École primaire	Cours préparatoire	CP	6–7
	Cours élémentaire première année	CE1	7–8
	Cours élémentaire deuxième année	CE2	8–9
	Cours moyen première année	CM1	9–10
	Cours moyen deuxième année	CM2	10–11
Collège	Sixième	6e	11–12
	Cinquième	5e	12–13
	Quatrième	4e	13–14
	Troisième	3e	15–16

Did you know?

There are also some secondary schools for pupils with special talent. They have normal lessons in the morning and then concentrate on sport, music, dance or drama in the afternoon.

MINI-QUIZ

Can you guess?

1 The number of hours French primary school children are at school in an average week?

- 15
- 21
- 27

2 The number of weeks' holiday per year for French pupils?

- 10
- 13
- 16

3 What are French schools often named after?

- famous people
- wild animals
- planets

MINI-QUIZ ANSWERS

3 famous people

2 16 (only 13 in the UK)

1 27 hours (only 21 in the UK)

EXTRA CHALLENGE

Which class would you be in if you went to school in France?

À L'ÉCOLE PRIMAIRE

Marie-Lou goes to primary school. Today she is telling our young reporter Ryan about her school.

Young reporter: **Quels jours est-ce que tu vas à l'école?**

Marie-Lou: **Je vais à l'école le lundi, le mardi, le jeudi et le vendredi.**

Les cours commencent à 8h30.

In France, children used to go to school on Saturday mornings and have Wednesdays off instead. Nowadays there is no Saturday school, and some schools have a half day or a full day off on Wednesday too. But this may soon change.

Marie-Lou starts school at 8.30 and finishes at 4.30. It seems a long day, but she has a two-hour lunch break (**le déjeuner**) and 15 minutes playtime (**la récréation**) in the morning, and again in the afternoon.

Pendant la récréation, je m'amuse.

À midi, je mange à la cantine.

USEFUL PHRASES

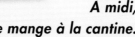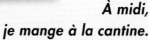

Quels jours est-ce que tu vas… Which days do you go… **je vais** I go **à l'école** to school **le lundi / mardi / jeudi / vendredi** on Mondays / Tuesdays / Thursdays / Fridays **les cours commencent** lessons start **à 8h30** at 8.30am **pendant la récréation** at playtime **je m'amuse** I have fun **à midi** at lunchtime **je mange** I eat **à la cantine** in the canteen

MY BLOG

What does Marie-Lou like best at school?

Her favourite lesson is English (**l'anglais**). She's been learning it for two years now and can say quite a few things. She is very proud that she can speak a second language. She has three 30-minute lessons a week. A special teacher visits the school for these lessons. Her name is Miss Hill. Marie-Lou really likes her because she knows lots of English songs and games that make learning English fun.

In primary schools near the border with Germany, they learn German (**l'allemand**). There are Spanish classes (**l'espagnol**) in the south-west of France near the border with Spain.

Marie-Lou likes learning judo best.

Marie-Lou likes PE (**l'éducation physique et sportive**) too. Every Monday, after morning break, her class goes to the local sports centre (**le centre sportif**). They do a different sport each half-term: handball, football, athletics, judo etc.

Days of the week

Monday (**lundi**)   Tuesday (**mardi**)   Wednesday (**mercredi**)
Thursday (**jeudi**)   Friday (**vendredi**)   Saturday (**samedi**)
Sunday (**dimanche**)

YOUR TURN

Et toi? Quels jours est-ce que tu vas à l'école?

Je vais à l'école le...

In French, days of the week don't start with a capital letter like they do in English.

13

AT PRIMARY SCHOOL

In France, children spend more time at school than in most other European countries.

If you are at a French school, you'll spend 914 hours a year in lessons. That is a lot more than in the UK, where children are at school for 846 hours a year, or Finland, where the school year is only 777 hours long.

Most time is devoted to French (**le français**) and maths (**les maths**), then PE (**l'éducation physique et sportive**, or **EPS** for short). Pupils also study a foreign language (**une langue vivante**), basic science (**les sciences**) and general culture which includes history and geography (**l'histoire-géographie**) and artistic subjects.

There are extra lessons (**le soutien**) to support pupils who are finding normal lessons a bit tough. They are usually 30 minutes long and are held at lunchtime or after school.

Did you know?
There are no assemblies in French schools.

How many pupils in a class?

It varies from school to school, but it can be up to 30.

Do pupils get homework?

Yes! Most schools set homework for pupils to do every evening.

What happens if pupils don't behave?

The usual punishment is writing out lines.

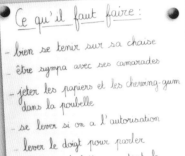

In this school, the class rules (le règlement) are pinned on the noticeboard.

Did you know?

In France, you can go home for lunch or eat at the school canteen. No packed lunches are allowed!

MINI-QUIZ

You might do these at a French school. Can you guess what they are?

1 l'appel
- taking the register
- going out at break-time
- doing a test

2 l'Instruction civique et morale
- cookery
- painting
- citizenship

3 TICE (techniques usuelles de l'information et de la communication),
- computer studies
- drama
- music

MINI-QUIZ ANSWERS

3 computer studies

2 citizenship

1 taking the register

EXTRA CHALLENGE

Compare your school to a French primary school. Find three things that are the same and three that are different.

15

AU COLLÈGE

Today our young reporter is interviewing Francky, who goes to secondary school.

Young reporter: **Salut, Francky! Tu aimes quelles matières?**

Francky: **Ma matière préférée, c'est l'informatique.**

J'aime aussi les arts plastiques et le français.

J'aime la lecture.

Les arts plastiques, c'est super!

In secondary school, there is no typical day. Lessons generally start between 8 and 8.30am in the morning and finish between 4 and 5pm. You might finish at 4pm on Mondays and 5pm on Tuesdays, for instance.

Each lesson lasts 55 minutes. As in primary school, there is a long lunch-break, usually one-and-a-half or two hours, to make it possible for pupils to go home for lunch if they want to. There is also a morning and an afternoon break (15 minutes each).

USEFUL PHRASES

Tu aimes quelles matières? Which subjects do you like?
ma matière préférée my favourite subject   **c'est** it's   **l'informatique** IT (information technology)
j'aime aussi I also like   **les arts plastiques** art   **le français** French   **la lecture** reading

Francky noticed a lot of changes when he moved up from primary to secondary school.

It seemed a bit strange at first. Luckily, it didn't take him long to find his way around even though the school is very big. Most secondary schools are much bigger than primary schools. In Francky's school there are nearly 1,000 pupils.

La musique au collège, c'est super!

Instead of having the same teacher for most lessons, Francky now has a new teacher for each subject. Most of the teachers have their own room, so he has to change room at the end of each lesson. He has new subjects too, like biology and geology (**sciences de la vie et de la Terre**, or **SVT** for short) and technology (**la technologie**).

Francky's school is very well-equipped. There are modern computer rooms, science labs and music rooms. Francky is learning to play the drums in music lessons. His mum is very glad that he can practise at school instead of at home!

School subjects

maths (**les maths**)   French (**le français**)   English (**l'anglais**)   PE (**l'EPS**)
history (**l'histoire**)   geography (**la géographie**)   science (**les sciences**)
biology/geology (**les SVT**)   technology (**la technologie**)   music (**la musique**)
art (**les arts plastiques**)   IT (**l'informatique**)

YOUR TURN

Et toi?
Tu aimes quelles matières?

 J'aime …

 Je n'aime pas…

French has two different words for 'you'. Use 'tu' when you talk to someone your own age. Use 'vous' for more than one person, or to an adult.

AT SECONDARY SCHOOL

At secondary school, pupils (**les élèves**) all have a special notebook called **un carnet de correspondance**. It is very useful.

It has their timetable (**l'emploi du temps**) and space for the teacher and pupil's parents to keep in contact.

It lists special school events and school rules, too.

If you break the rules, you might get a detention (**une heure de colle**). The member of staff responsible for discipline, absences and lateness is called **le conseiller principal d'éducation** (or **le CPE** for short). He or she is in charge of a team of assistants (**les assistants d'éducation**) who keep order in the corridors or playgrounds at break and lunch times. They also supervise study sessions if a teacher is absent. Often these assistants are students, not qualified teachers.

An English lesson

A science lesson

Did you know?

Most teachers (**les professeurs**) (57%) are women, which is similar to the UK.

Did you know?

In tests, French children always get a mark out of 20.

A French magazine asked some 12-year-olds what they would like to change about their school. The most common answers were:

- the timetable (most want a later start, a longer lunch break and a shorter afternoon!)

- the surroundings (most want a more colourful, welcoming atmosphere)

- the lessons (most want more subjects they can relate to and which will be useful to them in later life).

MINI-QUIZ

Can you guess the right number?

1 How many pupils are there in the average class in a French **collège**?

- 18
- 23
- 30

2 How many French pupils are absent every day?

- 0
- 5%
- 25%

3 How many teachers are there in French secondary schools?

- 200,000
- 20,000
- 2,000

MINI-QUIZ ANSWERS

3 200,000

2 5%

1 23

EXTRA CHALLENGE

Can you say how many pupils are in your class in French?

19

À MIDI

Today our young reporter is interviewing Léo. What does Léo do at school in the long lunch break?

Young reporter: **Salut, Léo! Qu'est-ce que tu fais à midi?**

Léo: **À midi, je mange à la cantine. Après, je vais dans la cour. Je joue avec mes copains.**

Like most of his classmates, Léo has lunch in the school canteen. He's not allowed to bring snacks to eat at break or lunchtime. Lunch is usually good and there are three courses. After lunch, he can go into the playground to play with his friends. They like to play 'tag' (**chat perché**) or swap cards that they collect.

Je mange à la cantine. C'est bon!

S'il pleut, je fais du coloriage.

USEFUL PHRASES

Qu'est-ce que tu fais...? What do you do...? **à midi** at lunchtime
je mange I eat **à la cantine** in the canteen **après** afterwards **je vais** I go
dans la cour into the playground **je joue** I play **avec mes copains** with my friends
C'est bon! It's good! **s'il pleut** if it rains **je fais du coloriage** I do some colouring

At Léo's school, there are special lunchtime activities, like football or **pétanque** (a French bowls game). The list of what is on each day is pinned up outside the canteen. Léo likes to join in these games, but he is also happy just chatting with his friends, or making up games with them.

Races and chasing games are popular. There is a funny rhyme made up of nonsense words for choosing teams or to decide who is going to be 'it':

There are quieter games too, like marbles or swapping **Pokémon** cards.

La marelle is a traditional game. It is like hopscotch. To play, draw this grid on the ground in chalk. Take turns to throw a small object and hop and skip from **Terre** (Earth) to **Ciel** (sky).

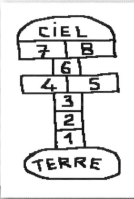

Amstramgram, pique et pique et colégram, bourre et bourre et ratatam, amstramgram! Pique!

Try saying that!

Popular playground activities

chatting (**discuter**)   football (**le football**)   tag (**chat perché**)
marbles (**les billes**)   ball games (**les jeux de ballon**)   hopscotch (**la marelle**)
card games (**les jeux de cartes**)   skipping (**la corde à sauter**)

YOUR TURN

Et toi? Qu'est-ce que tu fais à midi?

 À midi, j'aime...

To make a word plural, you usually add 's'. But with some words, such as jeu, add an x to make the plural.

un jeu – a game
deux jeux – two games

AROUND THE SCHOOL

Have a look inside some French schools.

La salle de classe (the classroom)

Léo's classroom is light and bright. Children sit two to a desk, in rows.

La cantine (the dining hall or canteen)

Lunch is self-service at this school. Children sit where they like, at round tables. Only two out of ten children go home for lunch. At Léo's school a meal costs 2 euros 90 (£2.40).

La cour (the playground)

Francky is lucky. At his school there are table tennis tables in the playground. Not all schools provide playground activities though.

Le CDI (centre de documentation et d'information) (the library)

Most schools have a library where pupils can find information for projects and homework, or just a good book to read!

Did you know?

In small country schools, children from different year groups often share the same classroom.

Les couloirs (the corridors)

Secondary schools often provide lockers for pupils. Here they are located in the corridors.

Les laboratoires
(the laboratories)

Some subjects are taught in specially equipped rooms: PE in the gym, music in a sound-proofed room and science in a laboratory (right), for example.

MINI-QUIZ

You will also find these places in a French school. Can you guess what they are?

1 l'entrée

- the entrance
- the cloakroom
- the sick bay

2 le bureau du proviseur

- the music room
- the gym
- the head teacher's office

3 la salle des profs

- the art room
- the staff room
- the caretaker's room

MINI-QUIZ ANSWERS

3 the staff room

2 the head teacher's office

1 the entrance

EXTRA CHALLENGE

Draw a plan of your school and label the different places with their French names.

LES ACTIVITÉS EXTRA-SCOLAIRES

Today our young reporter is interviewing Léo about the clubs and after-school activities at his school.

Young reporter: **Léo, tu fais partie d'un club ou d'une équipe à l'école?**

Léo: **Je vais au club d'escalade. C'est le lundi, après les cours.**

C'est génial!

Il y a un club d'échecs le mardi, à midi.

Il y a aussi une équipe de foot.

Because the school day finishes quite late in France, there are not many after-school clubs. Teachers do not want to stay late, and pupils need to get home to do their homework!

Léo is lucky. In his school, some teachers volunteer to run activities, like a climbing club and a chess club, at lunchtime and after school.

USEFUL PHRASES

Tu fais partie de...? Do you belong to...? **un club** a club **une équipe** a team
à l'école at school **je vais** I go **le club d'escalade** climbing club
le lundi / le mardi on Mondays / on Tuesdays **après les cours** after school
à midi at lunchtime **c'est génial!** it's great! **un club d'échecs** a chess club

MY BLOG
Léo does quite a few activities outside the classroom.

Léo is not in any sports teams but he loves sport. He has recently started going to a climbing club with his teacher on Mondays after school. And on Fridays, he and his school friends go to a swimming club at the local swimming pool (**la piscine**). He's a good swimmer and has already got his 25 metre certificate (**le brevet 25 mètres**).

Léo likes music too. Soon he is going to be in an orchestra. **Orchestres à l'école** is coming to his school. It's an

Léo and his classmates are going to the swimming pool.

organisation which sends professional musicians to French schools. They work with pupils who have never played a musical instrument before. They form an orchestra (**un orchestre**) and learn the music by heart.

Léo would like to play the trumpet like his friend Bastien.

School teams and clubs

football team (**l'équipe de football**)   hockey team (**l'équipe de hockey**)
handball team (**l'équipe de handball**)   orchestra (**l'orchestre**)
choir (**la chorale**)   drama club (**le club de théâtre**)   chess club (**le club d'échecs**)   judo club (**le club de judo**)   art club (**le club de dessin**)

YOUR TURN

Et toi? Tu fais partie d'un club ou d'une équipe à l'école?

• *Je fais partie d'un club de…*

• *Je fais partie d'une équipe de…*

Some French words look the same (or almost) as English ones. But they don't sound the same! How many can you think of?

GETTING OUT AND ABOUT

School trips can be great fun!

There are three important mountain ranges in France: the Alps in south-east France, the Massif Central in the south-central region and the Pyrénées in the south-west. In winter, some French classes go with their teacher to the mountains for lessons with a difference: **les classes de neige** (literally: snow classes). They learn to ski and try other winter sports.

Setting off on a school trip.

France also has some amazing cities for school trips. Paris is the capital of France and is particularly popular. There is so much to see and do! A boat trip on the River Seine is a great way to see a lot of the famous monuments, like the Eiffel Tower and Notre-Dame Cathedral.

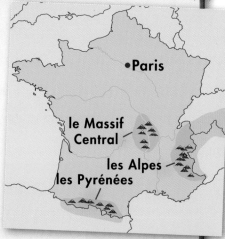

•Paris

le Massif Central

les Alpes

les Pyrénées

Notre-Dame, Paris.

In spring or summer, there are **les classes de mer**, or **les classes vertes**. These are school trips with a theme, where pupils learn about the sea or the countryside. Environmental projects are popular.

Une classe verte

Did you know?

There are some great theme parks in France for a school trip. History comes alive with gladiators and Vikings at the historical theme park **Le Puy du Fou** in the Vendée region. Or budding astronauts can learn all about space travel at the **Cité de l'Espace** in Toulouse.

Le Puy du Fou is a popular theme park in Western France.

MINI-QUIZ

Can you guess where these school trips would be going?

1 à la montagne
- to the seaside
- to the mountains
- to a city

2 à la mer
- to the countryside
- to the seaside
- to a theme park

3 à l'étranger
- abroad
- to a youth hostel
- to a summer camp

MINI-QUIZ ANSWERS

3 abroad

2 to the seaside

1 to the mountains

EXTRA CHALLENGE

Improve your geography. On the Internet or in an atlas, find a map of France. Can you locate the places mentioned on these pages?

TEST YOUR MEMORY!

1 When is la rentrée?

- January
- July
- September

2 What do French children wear to school?

- school uniform
- a special school T-shirt
- whatever they like

3 If you are 12, which school do you go to?

- l'école maternelle
- l'école primaire
- le collège

4 Do pupils learn a foreign language at primary school?

- no
- yes, usually English
- yes, usually Chinese

5 Do French schools have assemblies?

- yes, every day
- yes, occasionally
- no, never

6 What do most children do at lunchtime?

- go home to eat
- have packed lunch
- eat at the school canteen

7 How long is the typical French lunch-break?

- half-an-hour
- an hour
- two hours

8 Where might you hear the **Amstramgram** rhyme?

- in the playground
- in a music lesson
- in the head teacher's office

Look back through the book to check your answers.

INTERESTING WEBSITES

- **Read about class CM2 at a typical French primary school**: http://cm2degaulle.eklablog.com/bienvenue-dans-notre-univers-p33739 **and** http://cm2degaulle.eklablog.com/nos-activites-au-quotidien-c213306

- **Watch a short video about a school on the Caribbean island of Martinique (which is actually a part of France)**: http://www.teachers.tv/videos/lesson-starters-primary-french-bienvenue-en-martinique-2

- **Play games to practise your French**: http://www.bbc.co.uk/schools/primaryfrench/index_flash.shtml

- **Find out more about the organisation Orchestre à l'école**: www.orchestre-ecole.com

- **Learn lots of interesting facts about France**: http://www.euroclubschools.co.uk/page29.htm

- **Print and colour some French pictures**: http://www.momes.net/coloriages/index.html

Note to parents and teachers: Every effort has been made by the Publishers to ensure that these websites are suitable for children, that they are of the highest educational value, and that they contain no inappropriate or offensive material. However, because of the nature of the Internet, it is impossible to guarantee that the contents of these sites will not be altered. We strongly advise that Internet access is supervised by a responsible adult.

TRANSLATIONS

Pages 8–9

La rentrée Back-to-school day

Salut, Marie-Lou! Qu'est-ce que tu fais?

Hallo, Marie-Lou! What are you doing?

C'est la rentrée! Je prépare mon cartable.

It's back-to-school day! I'm getting my school bag ready.

Mon école s'appelle l'École primaire Charles Royannez. La maîtresse s'appelle Madame Mercier.

My school is called École primaire Charles Royannez. The teacher is called Mrs Mercier.

Et toi? Complète.

What about you? Complete the sentences.

Je m'appelle… My name is…

Mon école s'appelle…

My school is called…

La maîtresse/Le maître s'appelle…

The teacher is called…

Pages 12–13

À l'école primaire At primary school

Quels jours est-ce que tu vas à l'école?

Which days do you go to school?

Je vais à l'école le lundi, le mardi, le jeudi et le vendredi.

I go to school on Mondays, Tuesdays, Thursdays and Fridays.

Les cours commencent à 8h30.

Lessons start at 8.30 am.

Pendant la récréation, je m'amuse.

At playtime, I have fun.

À midi, je mange à la cantine.

At lunchtime, I eat in the canteen.

Et toi? Quels jours est-ce que tu vas à l'école?

What about you? Which days do you go to school?

Je vais à l'école le… I go to school on…

Pages 16–17

Au collège At secondary school

Salut, Francky! Tu aimes quelles matières?

Hallo, Francky! Which subjects do you like?

Ma matière préférée, c'est l'informatique.

My favourite subject is IT.

J'aime aussi les arts plastiques et le français.

I also like art and French.

J'aime la lecture. I like reading.

Les arts plastiques, c'est super!
Art is great.

Et toi? Tu aimes quelles matières?
What about you? Which subjects do you like?

J'aime… I like…

Je n'aime pas… I don't like…

Pages 20–21

À midi At lunchtime

Salut, Léo! Qu'est-ce que tu fais à midi?
Hallo, Léo! What do you do at lunchtime?

À midi, je mange à la cantine.
At lunchtime, I eat in the canteen.

Après, je vais dans la cour.
Afterwards, I go into the playground.

Je joue avec mes copains.
I play with my friends.

Je mange à la cantine. C'est bon!
I eat in the canteen. It's good!

S'il pleut, je fais du coloriage.
If it rains, I do some colouring.

Et toi? Qu'est-ce que tu fais à midi?
What about you? What do you do at lunchtime?

À midi, j'aime… At lunchtime, I like…

Pages 24–25

Les activités extra-scolaires
Extra-curricular activities

Léo, tu fais partie d'un club ou d'une équipe à l'école?
Léo, do you belong to a club or a team at school?

Je vais au club d'escalade.
I go to climbing club.

C'est le lundi, après les cours.
It's on Mondays, after school.

C'est génial! It's great!

Il y a un club d'échecs le mardi, à midi.
There is a chess club on Tuesdays, at lunchtime.

Il y a aussi une équipe de foot.
There is a football team too.

Et toi? Tu fais partie d'un club ou d'une équipe à l'école?
What about you? Do you belong to a club or a team at school?

Je fais partie d'un club de…
I belong to a … club.

Je fais partie d'une équipe de…
I'm in a … team.

INDEX

TEST YOUR FRENCH

Can you remember what these words mean?

1 une école: a school? a teacher? a class?

2 les grandes vacances: pupils? summer holidays? textbooks?

3 la cour: the classroom? the hall? the playground?

1 a school 2 summer holidays 3 the playground